This picture book is dedicated to the animal residents of D.E.W. Animal Kingdom in Mount Vernon Maine. Located on 42 acres of Maine woodlands D.E.W. is home to more than two hundred animals from aroung the globe. The following pictures are of the baby residents of D.E.W. Aniaml Kingdom and Sanctuary. Please come and visit when they are open to public. D.E.W. Animal Kingdom is one of Maine's great secrets and wonderful treasures to all animal lovers. Their website is www.dewanimalkingdom.com.

![Baby animal standing in an outdoor enclosure]

"The greatness of a nation and its moral progress can be judged by the way its animals are treated."
— Mahatma Gandhi

"Some people talk to animals. Not many listen though. That's the problem."
— A.A. Milne, Winnie-the-Pooh

"If animals could speak, the dog would be a blundering outspoken fellow; but the cat would have the rare grace of never saying a word too much."
— Mark Twain

"The animals of the world exist for their own reasons. They were not made for humans any more than black people were made for white, or women created for men."
— Alice Walker

"Four legs good, two legs bad."
— George Orwell, Animal Farm

"Animals don't hate, and we're supposed to be better than them."
— **Elvis Presley**

"Until one has loved an animal, a part of one's soul remains unawakened."
— Anatole France

"I have from an early age abjured the use of meat, and the time will come when men such as I will look upon the murder of animals as they now look upon the murder of men."
— Leonardo da Vinci

"Animals are such agreeable friends—they ask no questions, they pass no criticisms."
— George Eliot, Mr Gilfil's Love Story

"I think I could turn and live with the animals, they are so placid and self contained;
I stand and look at them long and long.
They do not sweat and whine about their condition;
They do not lie awake in the dark and weep for their sins;
They do not make me sick discussing their duty to God;
Not one is dissatisfied-not one is demented with the mania of owning things;
Not one kneels to another, nor his kind that lived thousands of years ago;
Not one is responsible or industrious over the whole earth."
— Walt Whitman

"There is no religion without love, and people may talk as much as they like about their religion, but if it does not teach them to be good and kind to man and beast, it is all a sham."
— Anna Sewell

"Animals are reliable, many full of love, true in their affections, predictable in their actions, grateful and loyal. Difficult standards for people to live up to."
— Alfred A. Montapert

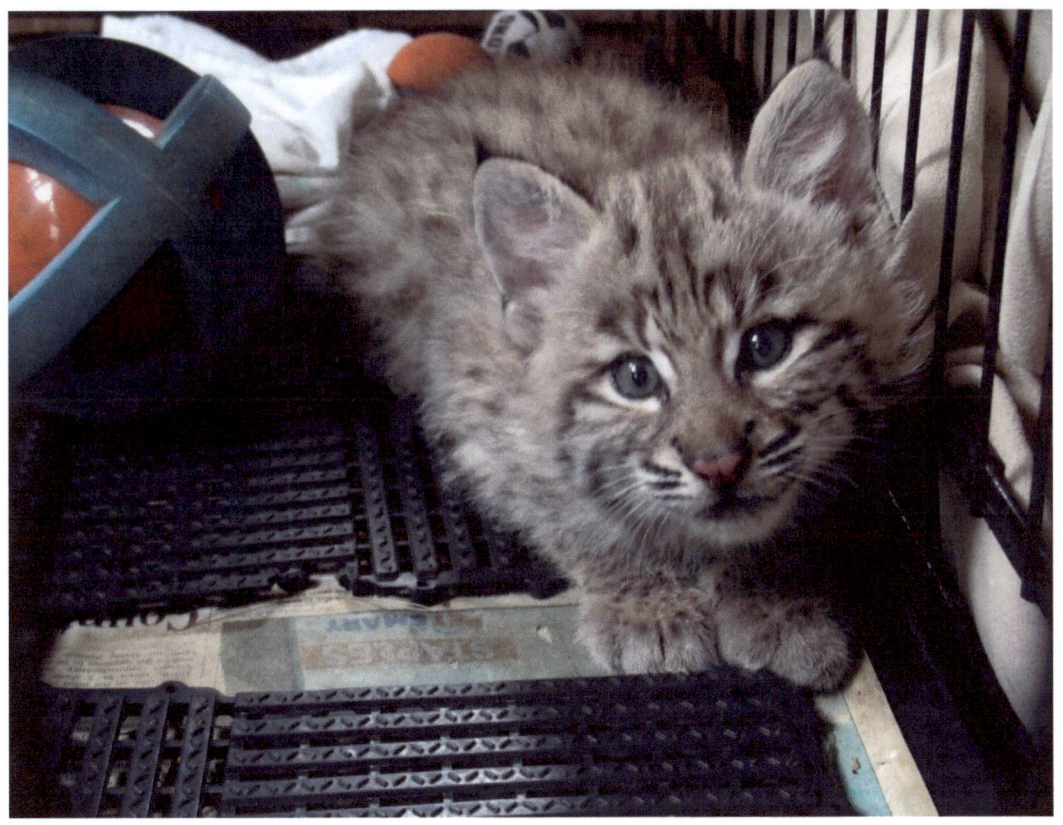

"If having a soul means being able to feel love and loyalty and gratitude, then animals are better off than a lot of humans."
— James Herriot, All Creatures Great and Small

"The assumption that animals are without rights, and the illusion that our treatment of them has no moral significance, is a positively outrageous example of Western crudity and barbarity. Universal compassion is the only guarantee of morality."
— Arthur Schopenhauer, The Basis of Morality

"How it is that animals understand things I do not know, but it is certain that they do understand. Perhaps there is a language which is not made of words and everything in the world understands it. Perhaps there is a soul hidden in everything and it can always speak, without even making a sound, to another soul."
— **Frances Hodgson Burnett, A Little Princess**

"Our perfect companions never have fewer than four feet."
— Colette

"Humans — who enslave, castrate, experiment on, and fillet other animals — have had an understandable penchant for pretending animals do not feel pain. A sharp distinction between humans and 'animals' is essential if we are to bend them to our will, make them work for us, wear them, eat them — without any disquieting tinges of guilt or regret. It is unseemly of us, who often behave so unfeelingly toward other animals, to contend that only humans can suffer. The behavior of other animals renders such pretensions specious. They are just too much like us."

— **Carl Sagan**

"Compassion for animals is intimately associated with goodness of character, and it may be confidently asserted that he who is cruel to animals cannot be a good man."
— **Arthur Schopenhauer, The Basis of Morality**

"An animal's eyes have the power to speak a great language."
— Martin Buber

"To my mind, the life of a lamb is no less precious than that of a human being."
— Mahatma Gandhi

"If you have men who will exclude any of God's creatures from the shelter of compassion and pity, you will have men who will deal likewise with their fellow men."
— St. Francis of Assisi

"We need another and a wiser and perhaps a more mystical concept of animals. In a world older and more complete than ours they move finished and complete, gifted with extensions of the senses we have lost or never attained, living by voices we shall never hear. They are not brethren, they are not underlings; they are other nations, caught with ourselves in the net of life and time, fellow prisoners of the splendour and travail of the earth."
— Henry Beston

"Love the animals: God has given them the rudiments of thought and joy untroubled."
— Fyodor Dostoyevsky

"Answer me, you who believe that animals are only machines. Has nature arranged for this animal to have all the machinery of feelings only in order for it not to have any at all?"
— **Voltaire**

"We must fight against the spirit of unconscious cruelty with which we treat the animals. Animals suffer as much as we do. True humanity does not allow us to impose such sufferings on them. It is our duty to make the whole world recognize it. Until we extend our circle of compassion to all living things, humanity will not find peace."
— **Albert Schweitzer**

"For animals that are overworked, underfed, and cruelly treated; for all wistful creatures in captivity that beat their wings against bars; for any that are hunted or lost or deserted or frightened or hungry; for all that must be put to death...and for those who deal with them we ask a heart of compassion and gentle hands and kindly words."
— Albert Schweitzer

"Hope was an instinct only the reasoning human mind could kill. An animal never knew despair."
— Graham Greene, The Power and the Glory

"Man, do not pride yourself on your superiority to the animals, for they are without sin, while you, with all your greatness, you defile the earth wherever you appear and leave an ignoble trail behind you -- and that is true, alas, for almost every one of us!"
— Fyodor Dostoyevsky, The Brothers Karamazov

"Love the animals: God has given them the rudiments of thought and joy untroubled."
— **Fyoder doestoyevsky**

"There is no folly of the beasts of the earth which is not infinitely outdone by the madness of men."
— Herman Melville, Moby-Dick; or, The Whale

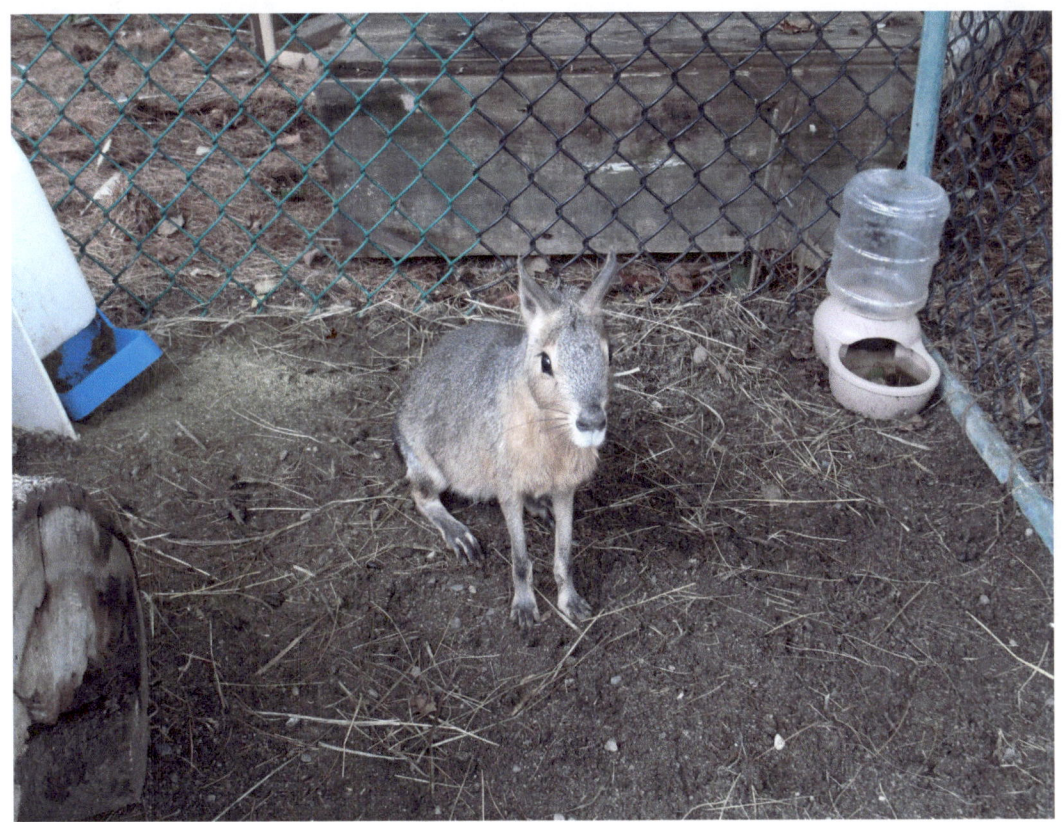

"Animals! the object of insatiable interest, examples of the riddle of life, created, as it were, to reveal the human being to man himself, displaying his richness and complexity in a thousand kaleidoscopic possibilities, each of them brought to some curious end, to some characteristic exuberance."
— Bruno Schulz, The Street of Crocodiles and Other Stories

"They do not sweat and whine about their condition, they do not lie awake in the dark and weep for their sins, they do not make me sick discussing their duty to God, not one is dissatisfied, not one is demented with the mania of owning things, not one kneels to another, nor to his kind that lived thousands of years ago. "
— Walt Whitman

"Besides love and sympathy, animals exhibit other qualities connected with the social instincts which in us would be called moral."
— **Charles Darwin**

"Animals, whom we have made our slaves, we do not like to consider our equal."
— Charles Darwin

"It is just like man's vanity and impertinence to call an animal dumb because it is dumb to his dull perceptions."
— Mark Twain

"A man can live and be healthy without killing animals for food; therefore, if he eats meat, he participates in taking animal life merely for the sake of his appetite."
— Leo Tolstoy

"I am fond of pigs. Dogs look up to us. Cats look down on us. Pigs treat us as equals."
— Winston Churchill

"The creatures outside looked from pig to man, and from man to pig, and from pig to man again; but already it was impossible to say which was which."

— George Orwell, Animal Farm

"I learned long ago, never to wrestle with a pig. You get dirty, and besides, the pig likes it."
— George Bernard Shaw

"Americans! They want to go 600 miles an hour, and they don't know how to walk! Look at them in the street. Bent over. Coughing! Young men with gray faces! Why can't they look at the animals? Look at a cat. Look at any animal. The only animal that doesn't hold its stomach in is the pig."
— Joseph Pilates

"Besides love and sympathy, animals exhibit other qualities connected with the social instincts which in us would be called moral."
— Charles Darwin

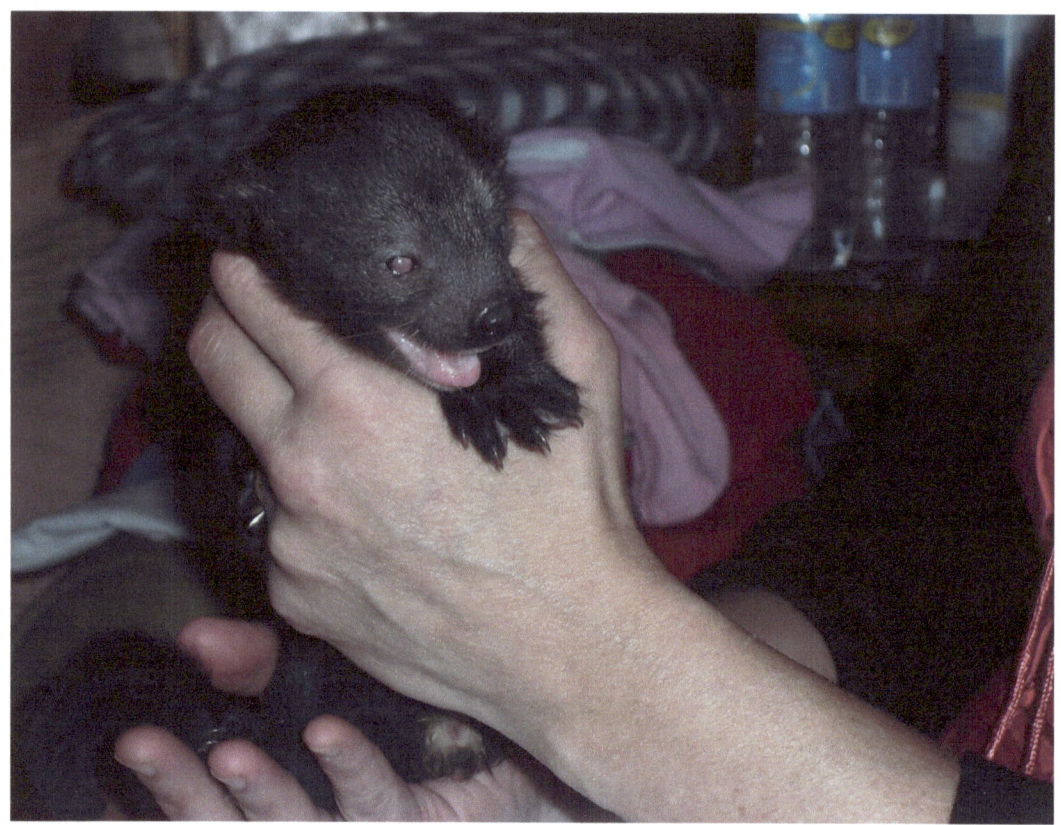

"The fate of animals is of far greater importance to me than the fear of appearing ridiculous."
— Émile Zola

"I never fancied cats much till I found the First Mate," he remarked, to the accompaniment of the Mate's tremendous purrs. "I saved his life, and when you've saved a creature's life you're bound to love it. It's next thing to giving life."
— **L.M. Montgomery, Anne's House of Dreams**

"The animal should not be measured by man. In a world older than ours they move finished and complete, gifted with extensions of the sense we have lost or never attained, living by voices we shall never hear."
— Henry Beston

"The mere brute pleasure of reading - the sort of pleasure a cow must have in grazing."
— Lord Chesterfield

"I am not afraid of an army of lions led by a sheep; I am afraid of an army of sheep led by a lion."
— Alexander the Great

"I have been scientifically studying the traits and dispositions of the "lower animals" (so-called,) and contrasting them with the traits and dispositions of man. I find the result profoundly humiliating to me. For it obliges me to renounce my allegiance to the Darwinian theory of the Ascent of Man from the Lower Animals; since it now seems plain to me that that theory ought to be vacated in favor of a new and truer one, this new and truer one to be named the Descent of Man from the Higher Animals."
— Mark Twain

"The day may come when the rest of the animal creation may acquire those rights which never could have been withholden from them but by the hand of tyranny."
— **Jeremy Bentham**

"The greatness of a nation and its moral progress can be judged by the way its animals are treated. I hold that the more helpless a creature the more entitled it is to protection by man from the cruelty of humankind."
— Mahatma Gandhi

"Compassion, in which all ethics must take root, can only attain its full breadth and depth if it embraces all living creatures and does not limit itself to mankind."
— Albert Schweitzer

"If an animal does something, we call it instinct. If we do the same thing for the same reason, we call it intelligence."
— Will Cuppy

"Animals shouldn't be hunted and nature shouldn't be disturbed, even destroyed, to benefit the whims of mankind"
— **Charles Manson**

"Results for "A man is like a cat; chase him and he'll run; sit still and ignore him and he'll come purring at your feet"
— Helen Rowland

"Love the animals. God has given them the rudiments of thought and joy untroubled. Don't trouble it, don't harass them of their happiness, don't work against God's intent."
— **Fyodor Dostoyevsky**

"Humans are amphibians - half spirit and half animal. As spirits they belong to the eternal world, but as animals they inhabit time."
— C. S. Lewis

Human beings are the only animals of which I am thoroughly and cravenly afraid.

— **George Bernard Shaw**

"While we ourselves are the living graves of murdered animals, how can we expect any ideal living conditions on this earth?"
— **George Bernard Shaw**

"A man can live and be healthy without killing animals for food; therefore, if he eats meat, he participates in taking animal life merely for the sake of his appetite."
— Leo Tolstoy

"It is much easier to show compassion to animals. They are never wicked."
— Haile Selassie

"All animals, except man, know that the principal business of life is to enjoy it."

— Samuel Butler

"As long as man continues to be the ruthless destroyer of lower living beings he will never know health or peace. For as long as men massacre animals, they will kill each other."
— **Pythagoras**

D.E.W. Animal Kingdom 918 Pond Rd (Rte. 41) Mount Vernon Maine

www.ingramcontent.com/pod-product-compliance
Lightning Source LLC
Chambersburg PA
CBHW041504280526
45792CB00004B/1131